Why Living Things Need...

Light

Daniel Nunn

Heinemann Library
Chicago, Illinois

www.capstonepub.com
Visit our website to find out more information about Heinemann-Raintree books.

To order:

☎ Phone 888-454-2279

💻 Visit www.capstonepub.com to browse our catalog and order online.

Edited by Dan Nunn, Rebecca Rissman, and Sian Smith
Designed by Joanna Hinton-Malivoire
Picture research by Ruth Blair
Production by Victoria Fitzgerald
Originated by Capstone Global Library Ltd
Printed and bound in China by Leo Paper Products Ltd

15 14 13 12 11
10 9 8 7 6 5 4 3 2 1

Library of Congress Cataloging-in-Publication Data
Nunn, Daniel.
   Light / Daniel Nunn.
      p. cm.—(Why living things need)
   Includes bibliographical references and index.
   ISBN 978-1-4329-5916-6 (hb)—ISBN 978-1-4329-5922-7 (pb)
1. Light—Juvenile literature. I. Title.
QC360.N86 2012
535—dc23   2011014650

Acknowledgments
We would like to thank the following for permission to reproduce photographs: Corbis pp.7 (© Randy Faris), 8 (© Kyle George/Aurora Open); photolibrary pp.16 (Imagesource), 17 (Ernst Wrba/Imagebroker), 20 (Fotosearch); Shutterstock pp.4 (© Juriah Mosin), 5 (© Milosz Aniol), 6 (© Evgeniy Ayupov), 9 (© Greg Kushmerek), 10 (© AnetaPics), 11 (© Darrin Henry), 12 (© hironai), 13 (© Koriolis), 14 (© Mogens Trolle), 15 (© saiva_l), 18 (© Netfalls), 19 (© Surkov Vladimir), 21 (© Konstanttin), 22 (© Juraj Kovac), 22 (© WDG Photo), 22 (© Richard Peterson), 23 (© Mogens Trolle).

Front cover photograph of sunflowers reproduced with permission of Shutterstock (© Vaclav Volrab). Back cover photograph of grass in sunlight reproduced with permission of Shutterstock (© Netfalls).

We would like to thank Nancy Harris, Dee Reid, and Diana Bentley for their assistance in the preparation of this book.

Every effort has been made to contact copyright holders of any material reproduced in this book. Any omissions will be rectified in subsequent printings if notice is given to the publisher.

Contents

What Is Light? 4

Living Things and Light 8

Why Do Living Things Need Light? .10

Light Quiz 22

Picture Glossary 23

Index 24

What Is Light?

Light lets us see.

Light comes from the Sun.

Light also comes from light bulbs
and candles.

When there is no light, everything is dark.

Living Things and Light

People, other animals, and plants are living things.

Living things need light.

Why Do Living Things Need Light?

Living things need light to see.

People need light to see.

Birds need light to see.

Even cats need some light to see.

Living things need sunlight to keep warm.

Lizards need sunlight to keep warm.

People need some sunlight to
keep healthy.

Plants need sunlight to stay alive.

Plants need sunlight to grow.

leaves

Plants take in sunlight through their leaves.

Plants use sunlight, air, and water to make food.

Plants need food to stay alive.

Light Quiz

Which of these things does not need light?

Answer on page 24

Picture Glossary

 **living thing** something that is alive, such as an animal or a plant

Index

animals 8

dark 7

people 8, 11, 16

plants 8, 17–21

seeing 4, 10, 11–13

Sun 5

Answer to question on page 22
The crocodile needs light to see.
The tree needs sunlight to stay alive.
The wooden blocks do not need light.

Notes for parents and teachers

Before reading

If possible, darken the room. Ask the children how you could make it lighter, for example, by opening the curtains, turning on a light, or shining a flashlight. What different sources of light can the children think of? Explain that the Sun is the most important source of light on Earth. Plants need sunlight to stay alive. People and other animals depend on plants for food. Talk to the children about the benefits and dangers associated with sunlight. We get vitamin D from sunlight but need to protect ourselves from strong sunlight.

After reading

• Place objects in a bag. Ask the children to take turns to feel an object and to guess what it is. Were they right? How did they check whether they were right? (By taking the object into the light so they could see it.) Explain that living things need light to see. Some animals use other senses so that they can tell what things are and where they are.

• Investigate what happens if a plant gets no sunlight with the children. Place one plant on a windowsill and another in a dark cupboard. Water both plants equally and observe what happens together over the course of several weeks.